My name is

• •

Note to Parents and Teachers

This book helps children to recognize and name different colours.
It also introduces them to lighter and darker shades within the colour
range. Bright, attractive pictures of everyday objects motivate young
readers to name the objects and say what colour they are.

Oxford University Press, Great Clarendon Street, Oxford OX2 6DP

Oxford is a trade mark of Oxford University Press
Copyright © Oxford University Press 1998
First published 1998
1 3 5 7 9 10 8 6 4 2

A CIP catalogue record for this book is available from the British Library

ISBN 0-19-910486-7 (hardback)
ISBN 0-19-910487-5 (paperback)

Printed in Hong Kong by OUP Hong Kong

My first book of colours

Illustrated by Julie Park

Consultant: Peter Patilla

Oxford University Press

red

red tractor, red face

green

green frogs, hopping race

yellow

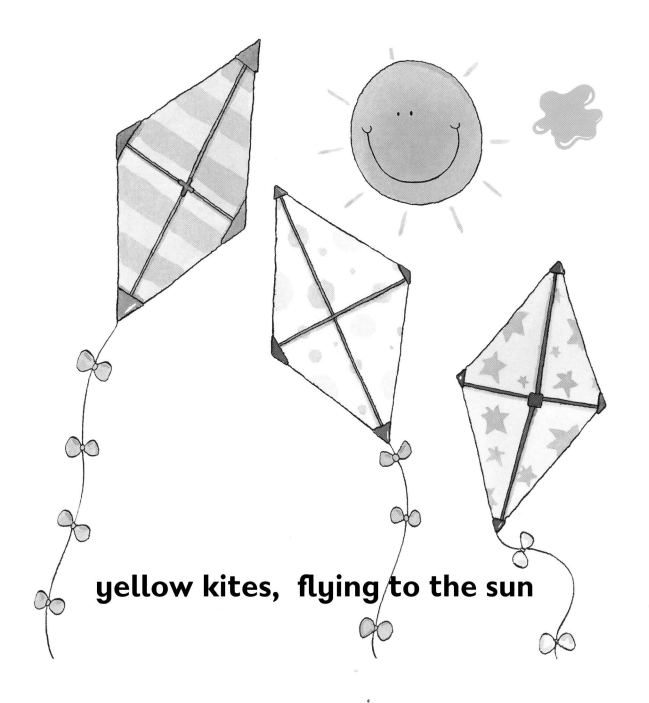

yellow kites, flying to the sun

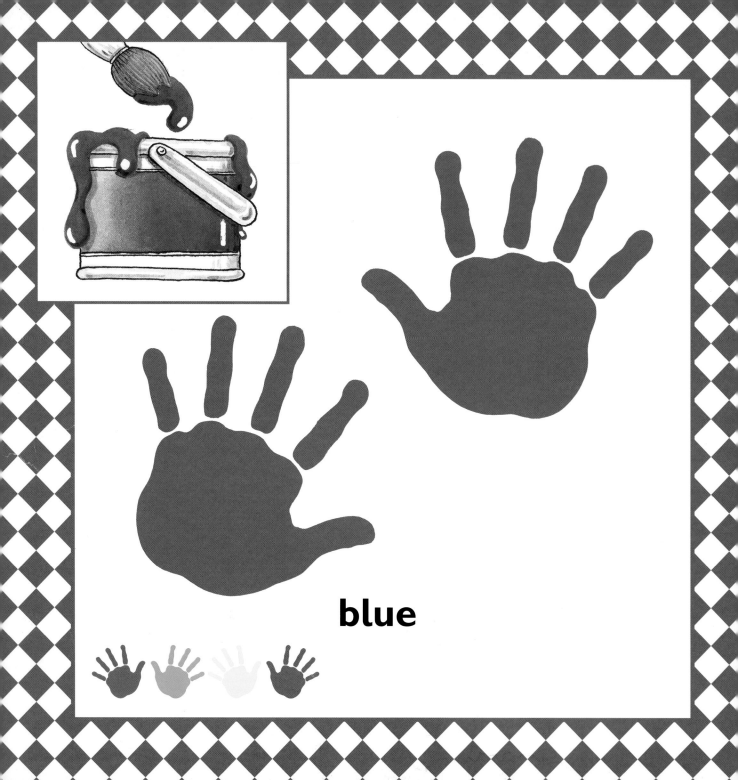

blue

blue fishes, having some fun

brown

brown bear, eating honey

orange

orange lollies, yummy, yummy

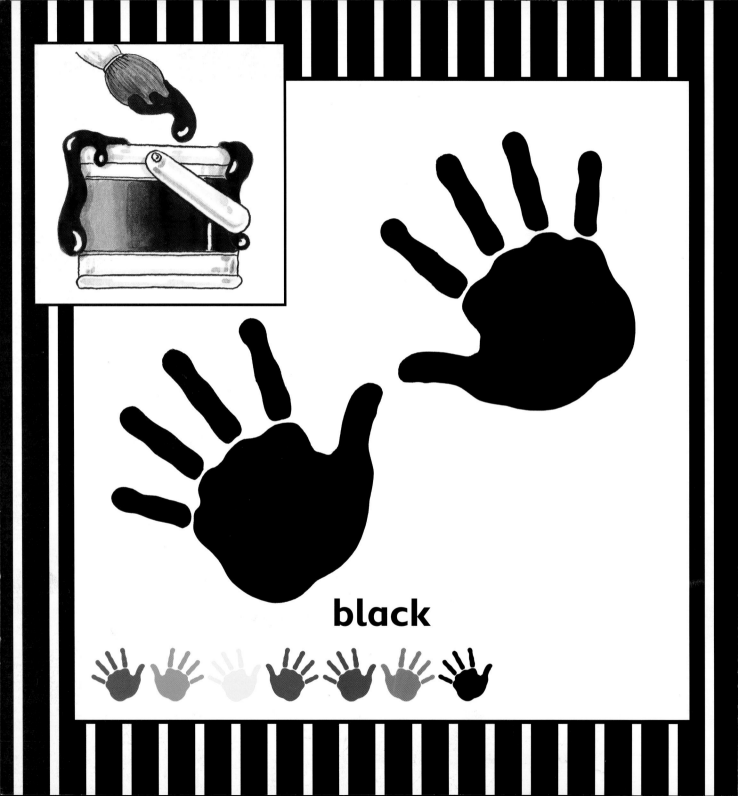

black

black spider, spinning web

white

white rabbit, standing on his head

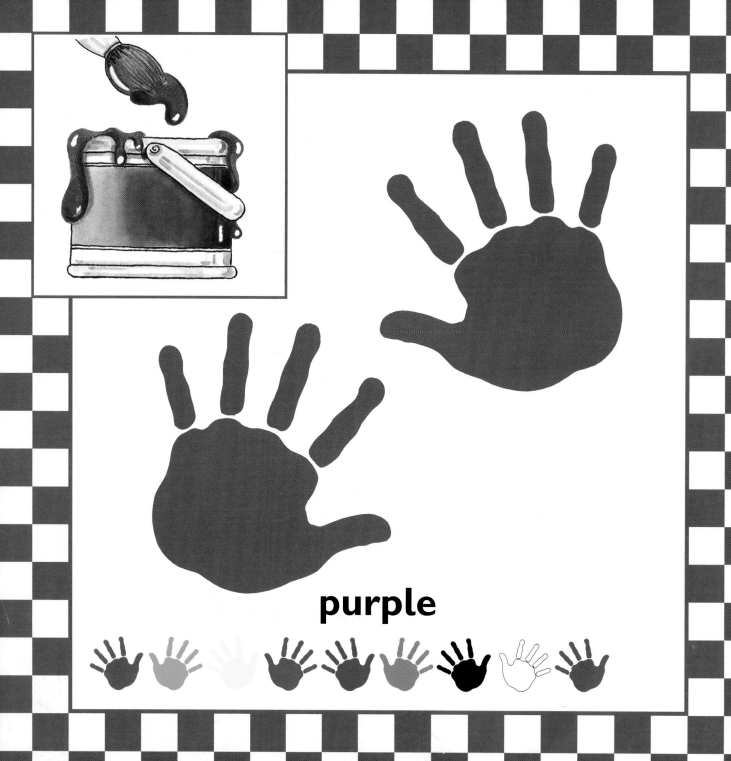

purple

purple bike, up against the wall

pink

pink flowers, growing very tall

red

green

yellow

blue

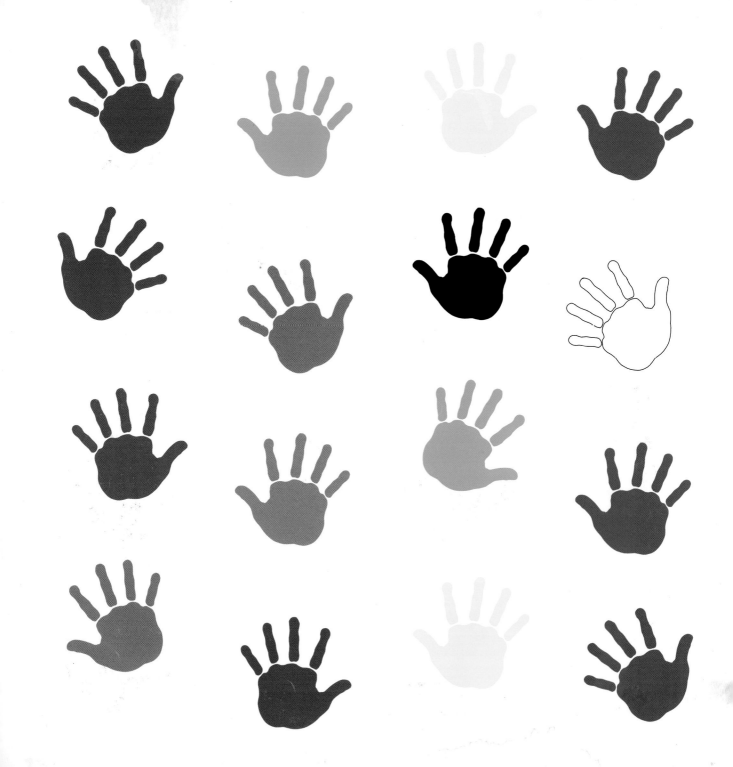